BOA
EDITIONS LTD

T0160991

I'M NO LONGER TROUBLED
BY THE EXTRAVAGANCE

I'M NO LONGER TROUBLED BY THE EXTRAVAGANCE

POEMS BY RICK BURSKY

AMERICAN POETS CONTINUUM SERIES, NO. 150

BOA EDITIONS, LTD. ◘ ROCHESTER, NY ◘ 2015

Copyright © 2015 by Rick Bursky
All rights reserved
Manufactured in the United States of America

First Edition
15 16 17 18   7 6 5 4 3 2 1

For information about permission to reuse any material from this book please contact The
Permissions Company at www.permissionscompany.com or e-mail permdude@eclipse.net.

Publications by BOA Editions, Ltd.—a not-for-profit corporation
under section 501 (c) (3) of the United States Internal Revenue
Code—are made possible with funds from a variety of sources,
including public funds from the New York State Council on the
Arts, a state agency; the Literature Program of the National En-
dowment for the Arts; the County of Monroe, NY; the Lannan
Foundation for support of the Lannan Translations Selection Se-
ries; the Mary S. Mulligan Charitable Trust; the Rochester Area
Community Foundation; the Arts & Cultural Council for Greater
Rochester; the Steeple-Jack Fund; the Ames-Amzalak Memorial
Trust in memory of Henry Ames, Semon Amzalak and Dan Amzalak; and contributions
from many individuals nationwide. See Colophon on page 72 for special individual
acknowledgments.

ART WORKS.
arts.gov

State of the Arts

NYSCA

Cover Design: Sandy Knight
Interior Design and Composition: Richard Foerster
Manufacturing: McNaughton & Gunn
BOA Logo: Mirko

Library of Congress Cataloging-in-Publication Data

Bursky, Rick.
   [Poems. Selections]
   I'm no longer troubled by the extravagance / Rick Bursky.
      pages cm. — (American poets continuum series ; 150)
   ISBN 978-1-938160-79-0 (paperback) — ISBN 978-1-938160-80-6 (e-book)
   I. Title.
   PS3602.U774A6 2015
   811'.6—dc23
                          2015019566

BOA Editions, Ltd.
250 North Goodman Street, Suite 306
Rochester, NY 14607
www.boaeditions.org
A. Poulin, Jr., Founder (1938–1996)

for Alan, the magic and humor belong to him

Contents

One

Two

Three

◻ ◻ ◻

ONE

The Relentless

One day we'll know how long
the dead have to be dead
before they feel hunger.
One day it'll be summer forever.
In the meantime, the weather,
looking for its cue, keeps an eye on me,
and I keep whatever money's in my pocket
crumpled in a ball. A relentless
responsibility dogs me, and the funny thing
is, these are the lyrics to a happy song.
Go ahead, tap your foot,
snap your fingers.
We're roasting a pig in the yard.

The Fear

Love without fear is meaningless; it's a machine
like grief, always in the early stages of invention.
I was once the human equivalent of a starfish.
Each limb torn from my body grew back.
But the world stopped performing triage on me years ago.
There's a new science developing here,
I just can't put my finger on it, or perhaps
this is a trick I play on myself, a survival strategy, of sorts.
How troubling would it be if I didn't survive?
Each night, my house catches fire, burns
to ashes as thick, black braids of smoke
assemble on the roof and push into the darkness.
Each night, I sweat into my dreams
and wake pale as the sky each morning.
Mathematics play a role in most forms of disappointment.
See for yourself, you can calculate everything, everything.

But First

My thoughts are as impure as yours.
And it would no longer be difficult
to memorize each others' every virtue.
My bones have not always been made of straw.
Each day is a slice of bread and we're free
to argue the significance of butter
and other temptations.
But first, we have decisions to make.
If you dance with me.
If we agree to fall down a flight of stairs together.
If we wore each other's underwear for the entire day.
When I heard you say
"we can do better" I wasn't sure
if it was a question or statement.
Is tomorrow your turn to blacken my eye?
In my next life I promise to be
something similar to a river.
We have one more chance to make cherry pits
our favorite form of currency again,
one more chance to prove
you can enjoy anything if you imagine
the right music playing in your head.

There Are New Games We Can Play

I once believed I could warm my blood
by making my heart erupt into flame,
once believed I could disguise myself
by turning my skin into a wall laced with vines
—but a woman convinced me otherwise.
You, on the other hand,
have convinced me of nothing.
So go ahead, pretend we're talking.
You'll tell me how the telephone rings
without being prompted.
I'll tell you how clouds form a map
only the dying can read. It's wonderful how
honesty is a convention so easy to malign.
Still, the truth keeps its secrets to itself.

Cloud Theory

for Vyvyane

No one gave much thought to the weight
of the cumulus cloud overhead
until it collapsed killing forty-nine people.
The weight of a typical cumulus,
a little over two billion pounds.
Notice "typical" and "little."
It's these nuances that separate us
from other animals. It makes me nervous
to think about the darkness inside my body.
What other animal would think about that?
One religion still insists
clouds originate as the dying breaths of angels
destined to be reincarnated as gods.

Scientists estimate the oldest cloud on earth,
an altocumulus lenticularis, has survived
two hundred eighty-seven years;
the runner-up, forty-two years.
The discrepancy is being investigated.
When I was young I kept three clouds in mason jars.
Came home from school one day
and they were gone. Years later my mother told me
my father flushed them down the toilet.
After making love to a woman
with clouds painted on her ceiling
I told her about the metal plate in my head.
She left me the next day. Years later she wrote
to say she also had a plate in her head.
This is how we learn from each other.

Only three species of clouds
are known to have gone extinct.
Perhaps clouds have more
in common with sharks than waves do.

I think I'm talking about courage.
Altostratus, mammatus, cirrus, noctilucent
—when I'm afraid, really afraid,
I quietly chant—altostratus, mammatus,
cirrus, noctilucent—and go to sleep.
Sometimes in the morning before work
I sit in my car, watch clouds gather
and the sky twitch like an eye
with something small,
very small, caught under the lid.

We Were Similar in That Way

It was windy in the snow globe.
Our windowpanes rattled.
Snow piled at the door.
We held hands and sat cross-legged on the floor.
We didn't know when the storm would pass.
Take whatever you want, she said.
I said the same. And neither of us took a thing.
After we let go of each other
I couldn't decide what to do with my hands.
She decided to run sobbing from the house,
into the swirling snow.
That was the last time I saw her.
Yes, we were once that small.

The Vocabularies

The knot in my chest, a doctor said, was a splinter
of lightning, x-rays weren't needed.
He said stand in a dark forest on a night
with electricity in the sky, soft light will glow
from the ears, nostrils, and mouth.
But I said a man should know his content.
Mine was a knot of barbed wire and string.
The wire once surrounded a camp.
The string held a yellow balloon to a birthday present,
though I don't know for whom.
Every time I say this it begins to rain.
Do you believe in ghosts?

This is what the doctor was talking about.
Heart isn't the only word in the chest's vocabulary.
Others include *knot* and *apparition*,
not necessarily a ghost, but the shape
a breath creates on a cold morning.
It starts in the chest.
A doctor covered my mouth with a mask,
forced every breath I ever took to return.
A woman covered my mouth with hers, the same result.
A breath has many uses; she said
she would save some for me to use when I stood
on the edge of a forest to light the way.

I'm No Longer Troubled by the Extravagance

I loved a woman with three arms.
Not that I required the extra appendage.
The two arms of previous lovers were always enough.
But three arms are an advantage
when it comes to carrying things
and love. The woman with three arms said
love was nothing but a grammar
for exploitation. The arm was supposed to be
removed when she was eight months old.
Her parents changed their minds
as she was rolled in the operating room.
Her third arm was a *coup d'essai* at faith.
For me it was an aphrodisiac.
She studied to be a juggler.
I studied to be an audience.
Imagine her in a spotlight
—a universe of oranges whirling round her head.
Now imagine a thousand of me.
Sometimes she was amused
by the gold goddess Kali I gave her,
other times she was angered.
At twenty-seven she was killed
in an automobile accident.
My heart is a rumor. A pair
of her shoes remains beneath my bed.

Another Simony

People mistake me for Jesus when I wear a crown of thorns,
it's an understandable mistake. It was a gift,
the crown of thorns, from a lover.
At first, she asked me to wear it only during sex.
Then the occasional dinner out.
A woman once asked me to wear socks
during sex, and not because it was winter
and the heater was broken. I didn't complain
because it was winter, the heater was broken
and sometimes my feet slid from under
the blanket and hung over the side of the bed.
The only person I'm interested in forgiving is me.
But it's harder than you think. I know
the Lord is listening over your shoulder,
I'm choosing my words carefully.
Did you know that virgins must wait in purgatory?
Did you know that originally
you were required to spit in your palm
before you shook someone's hand?
You can identify a sinner by how
they hold their silverware at dinner or perform sex.
There's a lot we can learn from each other.
Now you know how my heart became
the marching band following the coffin.

Love and Other Academic Exercises

Now I only remember you during lightning storms,
she wrote in a birthday card. I wanted to write back, remind her
of the diorama our bedroom had become, where differences
between a porcelain doll and person weren't always clear.
This was one of the secrets she loved, hid them everywhere.

She once wrote, you'd be surprised what could be hid
in a shed beneath a lawn mower's rusting blades, and I was.
There was a time every photograph we posed for
turned breathless and together we could make
the sound of a nail discovering a hole.

I've Already Said Too Much

An old man and woman live inside my heart.
I don't know what language they speak
but know they speak with an accent.
When I sleep they dance like old people
dance when no one is looking.
I promised a doctor I wouldn't discuss this.
Promised a lover I wouldn't reveal names.
Some things we know can never be explained.
I don't believe it's possible for snow to fall inside my heart.
I don't know if the old man and woman love me,
or even like me, for that matter.
It's late, once again I'll attempt to sleep.
I bite my tongue to keep my hands from shaking.
It's almost time for something to happen.

The Intimacies

I suggested sex. It was our third date,
intimacy would not have been unexpected.
She suggested we brush each other's teeth.
She delivered mail and I caught her
reading postcards on my porch.
That's how we met, how I like to tell the story.
The truth is she once was a stranger,
pointed a gun in my face, and demanded money.
I closed my eyes, counted to ten.
She was still there when I opened them.
The truth is there are more important things to remember.
On our first date she put her hands
in my pockets, leaned back against the door
and we kissed goodnight for thirteen minutes.
Some criminals have more patience than others.
She visited me in the hospital only once,
to break up, she opened the window
before leaving so I could enjoy the breeze.

All the Boredoms in the World

I forget if young girls still sleep
with their boredom beneath their pillows
until a boy says, I love you.
My mother planted her boredom
in a garden but never said what grew.
There's a pattern developing here.
No one is allowed
in the basement of sleep
but an old nun sits at the door
and sells postcards with a colorful,
but badly lit, photograph of it.
There are times when boredom is a hand
over a flame until the smell of burning flesh.
For miles that night, silverfish, dead, floating
at the surface, a piece of the moon on each.
I drove past people looking up at the roof of a bank,
arms motionless at their sides,
a staggering scene of languor.
It's always a warm afternoon
when things like this happen,
a man on a roof preparing to jump.

Though

Though she wanted to be a philosopher
and I wanted to be a philosophy.
Though she said earth is an experiment
and shovels are God's most honest angels.
Though the first time we had sex
was in the tree house.
Though she slept in my pocket
among two keys and a dark space,
and I slept in her mouth
with that moist wind
and the once-important warmth.
Though the truth is tiring.
This was an explanation,
and all night ambulance sirens
like hyenas circled the kill.

Experiments in Grief

I left the dishes in the sink for a week.
The porcelain bowl with a flower pattern,
now encrusted with yellow soup.
A wine glass shattered in the pile.
Peanut butter and jelly on white bread
and an orange for dinner. The kitchen,
no longer important. Grief,
in all its elegance, is the last and most fatal of emotions.
The magnificent way elephants grieve,
trunks the length of anger, tusks
ripping the sky—a woman studying elephants
wrote that in an essay, said she fed
them handfuls of pistachios
when they stopped wailing over the corpse.
I keep the curtains drawn. The passing
sun and moon change nothing.
Religion didn't invent grief, but raised it to an art.
A museum in Belgium, a seventeenth-century painting
titled *Grief,* a wooden spoon on a dirty table,
off to the side three wrinkled fingers reaching.
Sometimes, at night a dead elephant on my lawn.
Sometimes, at night a woman comes
and demands things. The wailing in the distance,
an elephant searching the streets.
Large dark shapes in the night aren't always the future.
Do you have to know what's on the other side?
The woman next to me on the train
had a padlock pierced through her lips.
Punishment is a flock of birds
dragging clouds across a gray sky.
But so is indulgence.
We each practice loneliness in our own way.

The Experiments That Brought Us Together

I commanded a squadron of yellow jackets,
a hiss or grunt dispatched
their obedience in pursuit of my bidding.
She commanded a towering cumulonimbus;
meteorologists felt threatened
when she shook her head.
What brought us together was knowing
that love is an experiment, no different
than filling a balloon with helium
and holding your breath until it disappears.
We discovered sex was a pain reliever.
More than once, I was willing
to pit my yellow jackets
against her cloud and vice versa.
But it never came to that.
What it did come to was her
wanting to throw a glass of water in my face.
What I wanted I kept to myself.
We discovered promise and divination
were synonyms and a form of currency.
Now let's experiment with mercy.

This Is Yours

I'm the most famous fabulist in a family of famous fabulists.
This was one of the things she liked most about me.
Instead of flowers I gave her a bouquet of full moons.
It was winter. We had sex still wearing our clothes
right there on the floor and pretended
we were in a snow globe.
I was flattered when she asked me
to take our wedding vows connected to a polygraph.
The things I liked most about her
were that she talked in her sleep,
wore necklaces made of thorns
around her breasts,
and the way we bled together each night.
What sort of relationship can you build on that?
Think Antony and Cleopatra, Hitler and Eva; oh,
I know what I'm talking about.
Who did Helen of Troy really love?
Who did she think of when she squeezed
her eyes and curled her toes?
You can tell this story
as if it were yours, even change the names
if you want, or call out mine.

Now I'll Begin Making Excuses

The sex smelled like lightning.
I didn't know if that was good.
She said, hold your breath until I return.
We loved the memory game
where everything has two meanings.
She said if it weren't for birds
there would be no sky.
That's one meaning. You create
the other. She's been gone
a long time; again, meaning,
last night I fell asleep
with a glass of wine
in my hand; even it spilling
on my bare leg or an angry bee
flying inside a balloon
couldn't wake me.

Notes Taken During an Arrhythmia

My soul is a black rag soaked in gasoline;
my bones, a rickety flagpole in the wind.
If language is a wilderness, what does this say
about the scrupulously worded truths?
One day you'll see whitetip reef sharks
ascending into a thundercloud on thermals.
One day they'll line the church bells

with the tongues of sinners
and we'll all sing along.
One day there'll be so much more,
but I've already promised too much.
The woman I loved most made a wagon
from my ribcage, used wheels from roller skates,
her dog pulled it when she brought vegetables at a farmers' market.

The Guerdon

Together, we're a map of a foreign country,
novice speakers of the native language.
Together, we're hands on a broken clock,
our mistakes public, predictable.
We're shoes hanging from telephone wire;
birds have their way with us.
Now let's talk about apart.
She adds pepper to every recipe.
I stop using the trunk of my car.
If love makes us better people
I refuse to believe potatoes have eyes.
She asks me to shower with her.
I lie and say I'm too tired.
Together, we're Rorschach test, furniture assembly
instructions—you get the idea.

The Pandemonium

The man with a wooden heart isn't afraid
of dying, but the occasional pain
in his chest bothers him. The pandemonium
of final moments, if he thinks about it,
makes him fidget. He'd rather think
honeydew melons on a windowsill, darkening
in a screen's threadlike shadows,
fits of sunlight, the sound of a knife
buttering toast, or how he enjoys strolling
to the mailbox for the harum-scarum expectation.

The man with a wooden heart eats at a round table.
Decisions annoy him, the way they dismiss
possibilities. At night he dreams of a woman
with wooden eyes that click
as they follow him to her bed.
She leaves the room to cough, tells him
fire took Joan of Arc, took everything
between her soul and the paper hat she wore,
burnt it all, except her heart, the size of his hand.
At dawn he reads crime stories to make sure
he's not a victim, obituaries
to make sure he's not dead.

The Nature of the Correspondence and the Required Heroics

The nature of a poem
requires an attempt at heroics.
A storm steps to the horizon and rattles
the sky each time you wake
from a nightmare alone in bed.

And the nature of a call to the heart?
The circus clown sits in the middle of a tent.
The bright red of the lips has worn off.
The big, round nose is missing.
He's playing spoons on his knees.
Civilization is a dance step
always in need of new music.

The nature of a pause, again,
this is about you.
You fall back to sleep
humming a song.
It's a false sort of courage
but right now any courage will do.

Every letter of the alphabet
was once a soldier armed with a pike
marching through a muddy field.
Read any story close enough,
you can track the letters back to the field.

I'm Telling You This Anyway

I worked winters as a night doorman in an old hotel.
I learned to open doors for guests
without allowing snow to follow.
Learned to sleep standing up, my face
in the official shadow of my hat.
Learned to wake at the first slowing sound
of a taxi's tire, opening my eyes
to green lights in the awning
glowing from each and every snowflake.
I enjoyed the cold, the way
it could smother someone's odor,
the way it could become steam
rising from urine pooling at the base of a streetlight.
Like all good night doormen I learned
to put the white gloves on
slow enough to feign importance.
There are so many ways to explain this.
I fell in love with a pickpocket, the cold nights
I found her hand in my pocket, holding mine.
Each night she disappeared before sunrise,
before the hotel detective arrived.

Cui Bono

There were years I did little more than study
the ambition of alligators in brackish water
and admire the virtuous speed of a bullwhip
at the instant it changes direction.
My first invention was something similar
to the music surgical instruments leave in the body.
All of this was satisfying but nothing
I ever invented could be discussed
in polite company. I asked a woman for help.
She asked less of me, or perhaps more,
this was never clear. For days at a time
we lay naked in bed.

When I told her I had to leave for work
she told me she was wealthy and paid my bills.
When I told her I had to leave for a haircut
she told me she was a barber and cut my hair.
What else could she have done?
When she went to the bathroom
I invented a more beautiful form of boredom.
When she didn't return
I invented a mechanical mosquito,
made the proboscis with a needle stolen from a doctor,
wings from her pantyhose, took wire
out of her bra to make the legs.
Though my invention never flew, one night
it walked across the bed, and stopped
between me and where she had slept.

There Were Indications That This Would Happen

She accused me of corruption.
She accused me of happenstance and mortality.
She accused me of plotting
our future one night at a time.
Such accusations. I tried to explain
how each wind on earth begins in a man's painful lungs.
Thank god for strong teeth, steel lips
—the damage that's possible. Through the entire dinner
the pressure in my chest, and I didn't say a word.
Candlelight sparkled on silverware
in a waiter's hand as he listened to her questions.
Imagine a constellation on the side of a butter knife.
I began to think of excuses that would allow me
to leave the table without looking back.
This is the last page of a novel I never wrote.
I loved her. Am I allowed to say that?
You should be taking notes.
In the backyard, the fighting cocks,
razors strapped to the claws,
were saying their prayers before the fight.

Qui Vive

Inside me, the burnt-out engine
she said was there all along.
Inside me, the trapdoor
I'm convinced is harmless.
Inside me, music, strings
played by women in formal gowns;
for the most part it's good.
I once was a winter evening
on the side of a mountain.
A string of climbers lean into the dark
and disappear into the distance.
Footprints in snow and the earth is flat,
the only way to explain
a marble ball motionless on a table.
Inside me, two crows cawing at a hawk
flying off with the dead body of a third.
Alone in the operating room, I lie
on the table and sew my stomach closed.
Rest, I say, slipping off my latex gloves
and washing my hands with antibiotic soap.

The Ending

I'm happy to report I'm no longer in love with her,
that my tie is a perfect full-Windsor knot
and I've renamed the large rock I drag behind me.
You knew all along where things were heading.
Once again, I'm returning to you. In the morning
now when I stand at the mirror and dress
it will be you, not her, I see in the bed behind me.
And I will think of myself as lucky.
Though my time with her was productive.
She taught me new sexual procedures, so you're also lucky.

I'm braver than ever now. Finally writing
that Russian novel about us.
You will be the forest. I will be the trees;
or even better, one of us will be
the crystalizing puff of breath floating
from blue lips in the cold, and one of us will be the lips.
On page 567, wearing only our underwear,
we will stand with dueling pistols
on a snowy Saint Petersburg evening.
Your arm will shiver when you aim at my chest.

TWO

My Uncanny Resemblance to a Young Sean Connery

Walking out of a Thai restaurant on Wilshire Boulevard in Santa Monica I was hit on the head with a wine bottle. It was night. At the instant of impact, a Santa Monica policewoman was leaving the See's Candies across the street. I didn't see the man who attacked me. The policewoman did. I didn't feel the bottle against my skull, opened my eyes an hour later in the emergency room. In the parking lot behind the restaurant my attacker put his hands behind his head and allowed himself to be handcuffed rather than test the discipline of the policewoman's finger on the trigger of her black Beretta. Doctors shined small beams of light into my eyes. Bursts of color. I slipped back to sleep. This was fourteen years after the collapse of the Soviet Union. My attacker, an unemployed Russian immigrant, claimed to be a one-time KGB agent, who believed early James Bond movies were documentaries. He decided on the attack when he saw me eating shrimp Pad Thai and talking with Alexis about the *New York Review of Books*. She was in the restroom when I was struck, held my hand in the ambulance as it carried me through the night. After killing an infamous enemy agent my attacker would return to Russia and find work with one of the many ex-KGB officers running a security company. This was real life, not a movie. The bottle didn't break. I spent three days in the hospital. After thirteen months in the Los Angeles County Jail my attacker was deported to Russia. I was upset to learn that the crime he was deported for was stealing the wine bottle and not what he did with it.

The Ring of the Fisherman

Imagine what the Bible would look like if photography were invented two thousand years earlier, or how photographs of Jesus on barbershop walls would have made his haircut the most popular in the world.

This is what I thought when I read about the Vatican's Apostolo Project: two hundred and eighty-one men in different corners of the world carried a small camera with them every minute of their lives in the off-chance God appeared to them.

None were ordained priests. All were Catholics of unquestionable faith. All met the pope, swore secrecy and kissed The Ring of the Fisherman. Only three photographs were shown to the pope, two in 1955, the third in 1996. This third photograph was the subject of anxious speculation among the German Benedictine nuns in the Prefecture of the Pontifical Household when one of them wrote to her brother that ". . . the pontiff sat in that straight-backed chair beside his bed for hours with the photograph in his lap . . . summoned his secretary . . . held the burning photograph over a bowl of water."

The nun and her brother, a school teacher in Verona, were brought to the pope, swore secrecy and kissed The Ring of the Fisherman. An outline of the gold Saint Peter dropping a net over the side of the boat could be seen on the brother's upper lip.

Mortal Wish

I was despondent after I lost my job as the sixth clarinetist in The World Famous Six Clarinet Band, spent weeks responding to clarinetist wanted ads in the newspaper before realizing that I was blackballed from the clarinet industry. When money began to run out I sold three soprano clarinets, kept the bass clarinet. Shaped like a lowercase *j*, I turned it into a vase for roses I stole from neighbors. The morning I learned that a member of The World Famous Six Bouzouki Band was killed in a fly-fishing accident, I traded a watch, two pairs of imported shoes, and an antique fountain pen thought to have been owned by an early vice president of General Electric for a used bouzouki in a pawnshop. An instrument to a true musician is like a fish to an ocean, or something like that. I taught myself to play so beautifully I could make a deaf woman selling shoelaces on a street corner cry. I later learned that experienced bouzouki players consider that a cheap parlor trick. I'm now the third bouzouki in The World Famous Six Bouzouki Band. Years earlier, while practicing the clarinet, there was a knock at the door. Still holding the clarinet I opened it to find a woman I didn't know pointing a gun at me. She fired three times. Two bullets flew wide. A third bullet would have entered my neck but first hit the clarinet. The instrument was destroyed but the bullet was deflected just enough that it barely grazed my skin. I hope to one day have that same sort of relationship with the bouzouki.

The Legerdemain

Door-to-door sales is a tradition in my family. My mother bought me from a door-to-door salesman when I was five weeks old. I've sold everything door-to-door—from silverware to poison, drank hemlock three times as a demonstration. Slowly closing the eyes is an effective sales tool. I was thirty-six when I sold my first tulip, a Red Emperor to a man on his way to a funeral, stopped him in his driveway. He held the tulip and sobbed. Selling tulips is selling desire. Other flower salesmen sell clichés. The tulip is a nightmare rehabilitated, closer to a human heart than a rose. Tulips are the ears of the dead. My work has hardened my knuckles. At the end of the day I sit in my car and watch the sun set in the rearview mirror. The Monte Flame is my favorite tulip, the way its orange and red petals cup every dirty secret you've ever told.

The Door

Each night a praying mantis abandons its camouflage and walks back and forth across my door. A door is easily confused by its purpose. The same way an attacking dog is confused by courage and fear. In 1737 thousands of praying mantises killed a woman pulling tomatoes from a vine. Flinging herself on the ground and rolling over and over crushed many but didn't save her. Dispatched by a congress of bishops, this is the first recorded instance of religious leaders using trained praying mantises for murder. The insect's natural inclination to stalk victims made it well-suited for the malfeasance. The insect's five eyes make it difficult for even God to go unnoticed. The spikes in their legs make everything else difficult. A door is one of earliest known prayers. The praying mantis that walks back and forth across mine spins its head, studies the moon, studies the doorknob, struggles to understand the differences. The man who found the woman killed by praying mantises first thought she was asleep under a thick green blanket that moved in the wind.

Rituals

Artichokes are the only vegetables that mate for life, though the idea of life in the sense of life expectancy in reference to vegetables is a subject of debate among scientists. It often leads to unwanted discussions about vegetables being conscious of their life expectancy and which vegetables have the ability to mourn. Many scientists, including two Noble Laureate biologists, refuse to go down this slippery slope and instead say that artichokes are vegetables of habit when it comes to mating. I feigned interest in the subject only because the PhD candidate telling me this was an attractive woman who I now suspect only feigned interest in me so that I would buy her a second glass of wine. The cheapest glass of Cabernet Sauvignon on the menu was seventeen dollars. She folded the slip of paper with my phone number into a long strip, wrapped it around her finger and joked that I gave her a ring.

THREE

The New Heroes

Tomorrow we choose new heroes by drawing names from a hat.
Each year a different man is praised for killing
a mountain lion with a rock, another for saving
a wooden Jesus from his burning house.
The annotators are oiling old, black typewriters;
unwrapping packages of paper and preparing for revisions.
The lighthouse keeper hasn't been seen since the last squall.
A woodsman has gone missing.
If their names are called someone will have to pretend.
The haberdasher has yet to open his shop,
but a crowd is forming to see the hat, dusty gray,
with words embroidered on a brim that no one will read.

The Accordion Player's Window

An old accordion holds it open on hot afternoons
and there's still space for a pigeon to fly through.
Sometimes he sticks his head out and yells.
Sometimes he just breathes.
The window was broken for most of last year.
Weather came in and on two occasions
a woman's hat. Both landed next to his feet
while he sat in the kitchen playing melancholy
songs about love and the resurrection.
He gave one of the hats to the old lady next door,
keeps the other on a nail by the back wall.

That Seagull

They covered their faces
with green paste, painted their bodies brown.
These were the men who became trees.
Other men became mountains,
convinced us blood no longer moved
through their rock veins
and sky grew from their scalp like hair.
Then there were men like us, who made
stories of what they could be and never were.

One man was a half-moon
flickering beneath a boat.
I could have been the rope
pulled taut against a weight,
a storm choosing a seagull to follow.

The Pity

1

After he shot the dog we skinned it,
grilled and pretended
the meat was imported and expensive.
Everything is easier to believe
sitting under a tree drinking
liquor on a Sunday evening.

2

It wasn't long before the damp grass
soaked through my pants.
When I sleep people think I'm dead.
The Greeks invented pity
to have something of value to sell
after all the slaves were auctioned off.

3

I pretended not to know why
he borrowed my revolver.
On the other side of the hedges,
I could hear a girl crying,
but it could have been something else.
Whoever looks at me while I sleep
appears in my dreams.

The Implications

A swarm of bees floated from an alley,
gray cloud the size of a car.
At night its commotion would be warning
enough but an afternoon city street,
jackhammer and stray sirens, the approaching
hum was ignored. In 1982, the mayor of Sassari,
a town on northwest Sardinia, was killed
when he sleepwalked into a swarm of bees;
the 247th most common death
according to the United Nations Statistics Division.
Some people still believe walking barefoot
through a graveyard's damp grass prevents syphilis,
something to do with the dead's urge
to procreate, an old wives' tale
stemming from the fact that a body
can have an orgasm up to nine minutes
after the heart stops. The implications
of requiring four matches to light a cigar.
The man standing at the entrance
to the alley would have gotten into his car
before the swarm of bees overtook him
if not for the time required to light his cigar.
Eyes closed, arms flailing, the man
in the center of a storm of bees
was afraid to open his mouth and scream.
Doctors in Italy stopped counting stings at 500,
suggested the mayor's casket remain closed.
The man at the entrance to the alley was not stung.
The three eyes of a bee see the world their own way.
The implications of a closed casket
on the soul's ability to ascend
concerned the mayor's mother,
holding a glass of cold water
in the priest's office.

I've Changed My Mind About Everything

I no longer mind if, while naked in the kitchen,
you bang pots and pans with a large wooden spoon.
I also have eccentricities. If you insist I stand
when I read to you, I'll think of Hemingway,
standing at the typewriter as he wrote.
I take back what I said about strangers
in our bedroom to create sexual tension.
While you stood in the dry cleaner's
I sat in the car and started to write an apology
but was distracted seeing your breasts
silhouetted by the sun low in the winter sky.
I was wrong to bite you, even though
you asked, wanted to apologize
like the pebble apologizes to the lake,
each ripple of water a growing remorse.
If success doesn't make me desirable, failure will.
Yes, I've received counsel from a career coach.
I'll make something of me,
or you, or you and me together.
If I seem presumptuous
it's the latest style in penitence.
Let's practice on each other again.
Let's prove what we take
from each other is worth the hate.

She Explained Me to Her Mother
Using Latinate Words

A love of handcuffs led her to a career in law enforcement.
A love of handcuffs led me to a career in crime.
The day we met. "Are they too tight?" "No."
She tightened them and smiled, and I smiled, too.
When I was seven I tied my legs together.
Love of handcuffs wasn't the only love
that brought us together.
A life-sized drawing of a skeleton framed
on our wall; pen, ink, red chalk on paper.
We both love anatomy.
When I was eight I stole handcuffs
and cuffed a cat to a dog.
When she was eight she stole handcuffs
and cuffed herself to a fence;
boys pulled down her pants.
Sometimes, just sometimes, I hear
her bones when she straddles me
and rocks back and forth.
If you have ten fingers you're normal.
We gave our bones new names.
Ulna: Man & Woman & Police Car.
Humerus: Now We Soothe.
I prepare breakfast on Sundays.
Anchovies, pancakes, sunflowers beside a coffee cup.
Medial cuneiform: This, This Is Our Moon.
She wore her uniform at my parole hearing,
was proud when she walked in the room
—badge, lipstick, polished nightstick, et cetera.
Red scars on our wrists like bracelets.
Clavicle: Oh My Darling, Tarnish My Tongue.

The Taming

I was a lion tamer for a zoo.
I studied to work in the circus but you know
what happened to that industry.
The preferred term today is trainer.
Some cultures say you train
water to boil, train your shoelaces to tie.
Cleveland, 1977, a 350-pound Siberian tiger
climbed its fence, killed a man photographing a child.
The Canchola Law, 1978, all cat breeds reaching
one hundred pounds at maturity receive
eight hours of training before exhibition.
Women find me unattractive until I tell them my profession.
The zoo lobby prefers the Canchola Law remain secret.
A 350-pound Siberian tiger is a kitten.
The first step in training a lion, become one.
To appear larger I wear shoes with three-inch heels.
My first wife was a professional dominatrix,
nothing but coincidence. The truth is
lions and tigers in exotic shows are born in captivity.
The same might be said for dominatrices.
I know what you're thinking,
our sexual activities, but you're wrong.
All the anger in the world evaporates
biting down on a whip.

And Then Empyrean

The ghost inside me shouts
into my dreams, claims if she weren't dead
she would be too beautiful for me.
Now I'm all she has.
My body is a haunted house.
A ghost could walk inside
forever without reaching a wall.
Another ghost swears he haunted my father.
When I ask about his last thoughts
dead breath blows across my bones.
My body is finally the shambles
that we always expected
—surgeons are sharpening their scalpels.
In the next life the great men will be snails.
Why some people are haunted
and others are not is something
scientists have investigated for decades.
A third ghost looks out from my ear at a pillow
and imagines suffocating me.
My favorite sounds are anything
dragged across the wooden floor.
Listening closely is how I learned
ghosts own the true franchise on empyrean.

Genus of Small Sounds

After the quiet years they invented a new way of singing,
began with the forgetting of words and small sounds that could be
      mistaken
for other things: automobile headlights illuminating the rise of a
      bridge
or a thick book's pages burning after being thrown into a fireplace.
Music was punctuation. A dying man falling to the ground
was a metronome. If his head swayed the chords were minor.

After the quiet years they turned a sepulcher into a lounge
where men wearing black silk shirts smoked cigars and leered
at belly dancers; so much time wasting itself, so much forgetting.

The New Skills

We abandoned the graveyards, buried our dead in forests.
We carved names, dates, and notes into tree trunks.
Thick roots twisting through the ground made our digging difficult.
Soon we began only to bury a wedding ring, or favorite sweater,
or a wrinkled piece of money with something written on it.
At first the gravedigger and the boy
who sharpened the edges of the axes were disappointed,
but other industries would soon hire their skills.
And we would hire translators to interpret the howling at night
that once we heard as only the wind pushing through trees.
No one asked about the corpses. It was enough to believe
that their new skills were also put to use somewhere else.

These Were Our Best Years

We slept better after we invented violence,
some of us resumed the habit
of muffling cries with newly plumped pillows.
We sang the same songs at funerals and birthdays,
served the same cake with sugary frosting, too;
occasions were sweetened this way.
We sucked smoke signals with deep breaths
and left the language to our lungs.
Then one night we opened the windows and doors.
Stray dogs wrapped in dark clouds wandered in.
What we couldn't see we could smell.

The Man in the Moon Retires
to a Small House in a Valley

A fleshless man doesn't need much.
At this point in life, the tides of emotion
could easily be replaced. Even a sound
would do, something like a cat scratching its box.
So he moves to the only place in the universe
where people swear they hear the sun approaching.
It sounds like it grows louder in September.
The groans of a distant highway at night
are meteors through the bedroom window.
Sometimes he extends his tongue for a taste as they pass.
He could be any of us when he sleeps;
the thin blackness cradles the skull's luminous horizon,
drool slides from the lips like small words.
Surrounded by mountains, it's precious.
The black and blue sky, it's precious.
Even the sound of the woman looking
through his garbage can, it's precious.
In the morning he wonders why he waited so long.

The Cairn

In the center of the brain there's a small pebble,
the sort that works its way into your shoe
forcing you to sit on the curb to remove it.
A coroner told me this in a hotel bar,
said it contains the same minerals
as pebbles on North Africa's Atlas Mountain.
Removing a bullet from a murder victim
is when she first saw the pebble.
Her report to the grand jury ended with an unlikely theory.
What wasn't reported was that the pebble makes us human.
An angel puts it under the tongue of each soul
before being shoved from the cliffs of heaven.
A little over 108 billion people have lived and died on earth.
I couldn't find an estimate on the number of pebbles,
though I want to say a little over 108 billion.
When I was in the second grade I made
a vase out of pebbles for Mother's Day.
Ten inches tall, painted it red, green, and blue,
I brought it home with a flower.
My mother keeps it on a window sill in the kitchen.

The Forest

I built a dark forest in a bottle;
used long tweezers, three glues,
and sixty-seven different materials.
I first saw the forest in a dream,
on the other side of a bridge
that took exactly sixty-seven steps to cross;
one step for each night Dante dreamed
of *The Inferno*. Cotton was smoke
rising from a smoldering fire.
Tiny drops of rubber became dew on leaves.
In the middle of the forest I dug a hole,
buried a half-moon made from Styrofoam.
With the sour breath of a dying man
I put wind in the trees.
Years from now a psychologist will swear
I was hoping to build a new start, will swear
the stains on the inside of my eyelids
contain a script, will swear
a dark forest can be surgically removed
from the imagination the same way
a splinter is removed from an atrium in the heart
after an explosion in a chemical factory.
But that's years from now.
Today there are lost footprints
that should never be walked in,
faces in tree trunks that trick you
into believing you know them.
Nightmares have no place in this,
the way they imply fantasy.
Time is subjective in a dark forest
in a bottle. If my forest was hell
the wax grandfather clock
in the bird's nest would have melted.
Cartographers mistook this fact for safety

and put my forest on maps.
Explorers prepared expeditions.
Before it was too late
I made a small Keep Out sign
complete with skull and crossbones.

Instead

We taught our horses to be wild, our dogs to shoot guns.
A sense of wonder marked our cowards;
a sense of resignation, everyone else.
Whoever pulled their own fingernails out ruled
with bloody pliers. The world was safer
once we understood it was against us.
There was talk of changing things,
but instead we put the faces of famous men on gargoyles.
There was talk of changing things,
but instead we repaired streetlights so they glowed
in the night fog like the eyes of wolves
who sat panting beyond the fences.

Acknowledgments

32 Poems: "This Is Yours";
Antioch Review: "The Cairn";
Conduit: "The Forest" and "Genus of Small Sounds";
Copper Nickel: "The Man in the Moon Retires to a Small House in a Valley" and "The Pandemonium";
Gettysburg Review: "The Relentless" and "The Implications";
Hayden's Ferry Review: "All the Boredoms in the World";
Hotel Amerika: "Qui Vive";
The Journal: "Cloud Theory" and "The Intimacies";
The Laurel Review: "But First" and "The Pity";
Nimrod International Journal: "The Nature of the Correspondence and the Required Heroics";
North American Review: "Experiments in Grief";
The Pinch: "The Pandemonium" and "That Seagull";
Plume: "The Legerdemain";
Southern Review: "The Accordion Player's Window";
Southwest Review: "The New Heroes";
Sycamore Review: "The Door."

For the careful reading of these poems, encouragement and company on the journey, so many writers to thank—starting with Alexis Orgera, always Alexis, there with words and wisdom; and Ian Randall Wilson who's had the pleasure or pain of reading everything I write, perhaps an apology is in order; Shivani Mehta for poetry every day; Nin Andrews and Richard Garcia for over a decade of support; Sariah Dorbin, there from the beginning; and, of course, Laura Kasischke; Lori Davis; Lisa Mecham; Becky Fink; Sanford Dorbin 1932–2014; William Burnside; Tony Caggiano; Peter Serchuk; Caroline Thompson 1980–2011; Rosalynde Vas Dias; Jay Brecker; Victoria Chang; Martin Ott; and Elise Suklje Martin.

Much gratitude to Peter Conners, Jenna Fisher, and Melissa Hall. This book wouldn't exist without their hard work and faith in the poems.

About the Author

Originally from New York City, Rick Bursky lives in Los Angeles where he collects fountain pens, works in advertising, and teaches poetry at the UCLA Extension Writers' Program. His previous full-length collections are *Death Obscura* and *The Soup of Something Missing*. He has a BFA from Art Center College of Design in Pasadena and an MFA from Warren Wilson College.

BOA Editions, Ltd.
American Poets Continuum Series

Colophon

BOA Editions, Ltd., a not-for-profit publisher of poetry and other literary works, fosters readership and appreciation of contemporary literature. By identifying, cultivating, and publishing both new and established poets and selecting authors of unique literary talent, BOA brings high-quality literature to the public. Support for this effort comes from the sale of its publications, grant funding, and private donations.

◻   ◻   ◻

The publication of this book is made possible, in part, by the special support of the following individuals:

Anonymous x 2
Nin Andrews
Armbruster Family Foundation
Dr. James & Ann Burk, *in memory of Dr. John Hoey*
Bernadette Catalana, *in memory of Richard Calabrese*
Jonathan Everitt
Gouvernet Arts Fund
Michael Hall
Chandra V. McKenzie
Boo Poulin
Deborah Ronnen & Sherman Levey
Steven O. Russell & Phyllis Rifkin-Russell